```
    D
    I
L O V E S
    I
    N
    E
```

A Medley Of Lyric Musings

David Arkell

Divine Loves

First published in Great Britain in 2019 by
CZ Design & Print, Southmill Trading Centre,
Bishop's Stortford, Hertfordshire CM23 2DY.
www.czdesignandprint.co.uk

ISBN 978-0-9956107-7-4

Copyright © 2019 David Arkell

All rights reserved. No part of this publication may be reproduced, stored in, or introduced into a retrieval system, or transmitted, in any form, or by any means (electrical, mechanical, photocopying, recording or otherwise) without the prior written permission of the publisher.

A catalogue copy of this book is available from the British Library.

Printed by CZ Design & Print, Bishop's Stortford.
Bound by Burroughs Print Finishing, Bury St Edmunds.

Scripture quotations are taken from The Holy Bible, New International Version®, NIV®, copyright ©1973, 1978, 1984, 2011 by Biblica, Inc.® Used by permission. All rights reserved.

All proceeds from this book will go to supporting the work of the Bible Society. Founded in 1804 and now operating in over 200 countries, the Bible Society is a charity on a global mission to bring the Bible to life for every man, woman and child, in the belief that when people engage with the Bible, lives can change for good. For more information and to make a donation, please visit the website: www.biblesociety.org.uk
Alternatively, a cheque payable to Bible Society can be sent to:
Bible Society, Stonehill Green, Westlea, Swindon SN5 7DG.

Contents

Introduction   5

Poems

Majesty	6
Divine Loves	9
Sylvan Scape	10
Shadowland	12
Liquid Lament	14
Swiftness Never Ceasing	16
Unwrapped	18
Cleaving	20
Vitality	22
Piano	24
Out of this World	26
Cornucopia	28
Borderland	30
Once for All	31
Destitution to Restitution	32
Sea of Love	34
Forever	36
L	38
Llandaff Cathedral	39
Evensong	40
Pentecost	42
Ladybird	44
River	46
Transience	48
Vision	50
Spacious Salvation	52
Stranded	54
Arcadia	56
Terminus	58

Free	60
Bombshell	62
Standing Firm	64
L'Île de Beauté	66
Reflection	68
Dishwasher Ditty	70
Blessed are the Poor	72
Apple Crumble in Heaven	74
Versus	76
Exhilaration	78
Broken	80
On Top of the World	82
Aware	84
Final Curtain	86
Just a Second	90
Fall and Rise	90
Dying to Live	92
More than Conquerors	95
Boundless	98
Being	99
Breakout	100
Transplant	102
Pilgrim	104
Index of Titles	106
Index of First Lines	108
Acknowledgements	109
Biography	110

Introduction

'From the heart, may it go to the heart.' Beethoven

How did it all start? On a dark January morning in 2011 I woke up early to the strange experience of rhymed lines appearing in my mind, and within a couple of hours six quatrains were formed. It was baffling, but I went with the flow, writing down the material and moulding it into shape. After the initial impetus long periods passed before new poems were born, and then the output gradually became more regular. The spark of inspiration is varied: a person, a Bible verse, an image, the natural world, death, love, music, time, pain, the Christian faith and God.

I find the satisfaction of writing lies in playing with words, meanings and rhymes, whose organic nature is stimulating and sometimes challenging, especially when a poem refuses to settle down neatly into its final form.

Many of the lines contain quotes from the Bible which are referenced in the footnotes. In some poems the word *Selah* is placed in a gap. This Hebrew term occurs in the Psalms, and one of its functions could be to indicate a moment of pause and reflection; this is my intention in using it, where it also serves as a bridge between two sections of different tone.

May these poems speak to you in the 'hushed casket of your soul.'
  Keats

David Arkell

'Yours, O Lord, is the greatness and the power and the glory and the majesty and the splendour, for everything in heaven and earth is Yours. Everything comes from You, and we have given You only what comes from Your hand.'
  1 Chronicles 29.11&14

Majesty

Gates of heaven open wide,
Saints behold the wondrous sight;
Now from earthly bonds untied,
Dazzled by the radiant light.

Thousand voices lift their praise,
Millions more join the throng;
Countless souls through endless days
Worship Him with joyful song.

Angels dance in jubilant crowd,
Clothed in raiment gleaming white;
Music's beauty chiming loud,
Rising to euphoric height;

Rushing wings upwards fly
To Him upon the throne,
There to hail and magnify;[1]
Hallowed name, He alone

Holds the true authority;[2]
Sovereign, worthy, just and kind.
Righteous in His sanctity,
None like Him can e'er one find.[3]

Maker of all, Eternal Now,
King of kings, Lord of lords;[4]
Every knee to Him shall bow.[5]
Celestial bodies by Him caused,

1. Revelation 5.11-13
2. Colossians 2.10
3. 2 Samuel 7.22
4. Revelation 19.16
5. Philippians 2.10

Issued forth and foreordained,
Surely moving on their round;
Universe by Him sustained[6]
Journeys, destined, onward-bound.

Comets, stars, gigantic masses,
Saturn's rings, plumes of dust;
Planets, moons, cosmic gases
Hurtling in expansive thrust.

Infinite time, measureless space,
Vastness of eternity;
Existence spans across the face
Of Love's resounding certainty.

Before the wonders of Thy hand,
Amazed, astonished, astounded,
Speechless, awestruck, here we stand,
Mercy's tender depth unsounded.

Lord, we come in trepidation,
Overwhelmed by godly might,
Humbled in our exultation.
Cast away the fearful night,

Rescue us from harmful blight,
Thou and we attuned as one;
Transformation pure and bright,
Gazing at Thy splendid Son.

Rays of gentle warmth and care,
Healing brought to every part;
Richest grace beyond compare
Reaching out to touch the heart.

---

6. Hebrews 1.3

El Shaddai, Spirit, Son,
Bathed in holy incandescence;[7]
Bring to end the work begun,[8]
Future, past, steadfast Presence.

Father God of highest renown,
Your Prince of peace[9] such peril faced;
Driven by love, to Earth come down,
All our woes and grief embraced.

Sacrificing self for death,
Pain exceeding comprehension;
Scourged and nailed, bled, bereft,
Purchasing complete redemption.[10]

How much the cost for You to give
Your one and only treasured Son?[11]
Life laid down saves humankind; with
Gasping breath speaks, 'It is done.'[12]

Hounds of hell with swiftest feet
Dash towards the tolling knell;
Satan's stronghold cannot keep
The Crucified in darkest dell.

Triumph of the resurrection,
Witness to the force divine;
Ours the boon and sweet affection,
Thankfulness an offering fine.

Perfect bond of Trinity,
Yours the first and greatest story;
Three in One and One in Three,
Scene of everlasting glory!

7. Isaiah 6.3
8. Philippians 1.6
9. Isaiah 9.6
10. Hebrews 9.12
11. John 3.16
12. John 19.30

Divine Loves

What is this thing that we call love?
How can I give it voice?
Flights of song on wings of dove,
Heart's elated cry, 'Rejoice!'[1]

Spirit's ardent longing deep
Soaring up towards the heights;
Fears and tears in flowing weep,
Aching pine for new-found sights,

Tones mellifluous, soulful eyes;
Racing thoughts in cauldron churn,
Aspiration's cherished prize,
Surging waves of constant yearn.

What is this thing that we call love?
A miracle of life.
In Him Who reigns in heaven above
I trust amidst the strife.

He knows the plans He has for me,[2]
In this I do believe;
That He my hopes and dreams can see,
I scarcely can conceive.

My Friend, my Lord, how great Thou art,[3]
My ever-streaming Strength;
Your matchless love will ne'er depart,
Such are its breadth and length.[4]

---

1. Philippians 4.4
2. Jeremiah 29.11
3. Psalm 86.10
4. Ephesians 3.18

Sylvan Scape

Bluebells spread out far and wide
Captivate with charm's allure;
Scent enchanting, beauty eyed,
Placid pose of calm demure.

Florid ferns in verdant glade,
Tranquil trails, lisping leaves.
Sunlight darts amongst the shade,
All blends well in quiet ease.

Birds whose tune bursts forth in flight,
Sing for all their heart is worth;
Élan's rise to lightful height,
Swooping down towards the earth.

Scurrying squirrels, docile does,
Furtive foxes, badgers bumbling;
Sniffling, snuffling, following nose,
Off they go leisurely lumbering.

Circling buzzard borne by breeze,
Grace of movement, wings full-spanned,
High above the swaying trees,
Roaming free on updraughts fanned.

Creaking boughs, branches' arch,
Canopies green cover and climb.
Stout trunks, slim ones, oak, larch,
Smooth, gnarled, ruffled by time.

Autumn comes, leaves transform,
Crispy orange, yellow, brown;
Cushioned, damp forest floor
Inherits foliage floating down.

Lord, I thank You as I wander;
Scenes idyllic, time to muse,
Contemplate both near and yonder,
Gaze, reflect, admire the views.

Ceaseless wonder, such variety,
Spellbound You do me enthral;
Rich abundance – what diversity!
Yours the hand that made it all.

Shadowland

Empty plains of hours stretch long,
Time suspended, almost frozen.
Wished-for sounds of daylight's song,
Stasis melting into motion.

Shredded reality, wispy dreams
Swirling in chaotic profusion;
Half-asleep, half-awake, it seems
The world dissolves in confusion.

Heavy mass of darkness stays,
Leaden in its clinging grasp;
Where to find the hidden rays,
Shining beacon breaking clasp?

Niggles lurk in churned-up past,
Disappointments' bitter bane;
Paths untaken, shadows cast,
Stifling weight of fate's disdain.

Hopes abound of what may be,
Prospects, plans for dawning task.
Problems, doubts, uncertainty,
Questions which I dare not ask.

Restless silence, anxious thoughts,
Ever-growing, rushing round;
Quell the misspent words, retorts,
Mindful breaths' repose refound.

If only eyes would gently close,
Leave this tortured place behind;
Journey on to restful doze
Pacifying body and mind.

Fresh perspectives take strange form,
Endless in their shapes and schemes;
Waiting birth of bright, new morn
Opening up to novel scenes.

At last the nascent gleams appear,
Driving back the tide of night;
Weary heart relieved by cheer,
Blackness giving way to light.

Grant, I pray, contented sleep,
Stillness of the soul restored;
Hold me in Your sheltered keep,[1]
Shepherd, Saviour, loving Lord.

---

1. Psalm 4.8

Liquid Lament

Welling up from deep within,
Whence they come a mystery;
Realms beneath the conscious rim,
Billows rock emotions' sea,

Dissipating rueful past:
Dormant passions smoulder, linger;
Broken friendships meant to last,
Love unbloomed quenched to cinder.

How long, Lord, can this endure?
Streams of sorrow pouring out,
Undiscovered depths obscure,
Existential fear and doubt.

Pulsing pressure in watery eyes,
Feelings dazed in fluid blur;
Pulled by currents of wishful sighs,
Groping for spark of light to stir

Soul's momentum, sense of meaning
On the winding pilgrim tread;
Opening the heart to fullness of healing,
Ousting self-pity with purpose instead.

Flowing relief of drops to ground
Melting pent-up ache away,
Sprinkling seed of dreams uncrowned;
Calm appeasing stormy spray.

Eyes affixed on heaven's prize,[1]
Freedom's nimble step in dance;
Springs of living water rise,[2]
Vigour freshly sown implants.

Life's far-reaching, fickle ways,
Changing with surprising faces.
Yours the constant, watchful gaze,[3]
Through the darkest hours and places;

Nothing, Lord, from You is hidden,[4]
Secrets all are known to Thee.[5]
Richly blessed or distress-ridden,
Every path You walk with me.

1. Philippians 3.14
2. Revelation 7.17
3. Psalm 121.3-8
4. Psalm 139.13-15
5. Psalm 44.21

Swiftness Never Ceasing[1]

Mighty pillars, towering, bold,
Lofty arching dome uphold
Of time's consistent, sweeping span,
Circling all that once began,

Which one day will its ending meet
When Chronos must concede defeat;
Finite mortals in humility
Recognise divine infinity.

Primeval forces clash, converge,
Miasmic mists dilate, diverge,
Bursting out new paths to trace,
Vastness black of silent space.

Just imagine the very first dawn,
Glimmers of light birthing morn;
Sparks of existence flicker, pulsate,
Alpha loosing aeons in spate.

Epic course of ages' movements
Fabricating nature's elements;
Swirling mass of starlit spheres
Unconstrained by months and years.

Millennia pass as Earth takes form,
Place and home for Man to spawn.
Striving to grasp in futile plight
Time's elusive, hasty flight;

Relentless advance thwarting attempts
Of those who seek to tether its ends;
Stubborn refusal to be contained,
Reversed, pushed on, changed, detained.

1. *Polyhymnia* – George Peele

Grip of the past, clenching hold,
Memories' treasure, loss untold;
Stories relived, imagined, spent,
Loitering threads of discontent.

Gift of the present opened today,
Cherished, enjoyed in finest array;
Golden moments never the same,
Though we long for them again.

Lure of future's dreams and fancies,
Panoramic possibilities;
Potent desires for what may be,
Wrestling with stark reality.

He of nature steadfast reigns,[2]
Compassing time in all its frames;
Past to present, future's land
Rest secure in palm of hand;[3]

Everything held by Him together,[4]
Beyond all bounds and thoughts' endeavour.
Ageless Source of life immutable,
Transcendental Being – beautiful!

---

2. Hebrews 13.8; Revelation 11.15-17
3. Psalm 31.15; 102.25
4. Colossians 1.17

Unwrapped

Father sent His only Son
To save a world in mire drowning;[1]
Reconciling work begun,[2]
Leading to His triumph crowning.

Tiny arms stretch out so thin
That one day on a cross will bear
All the suffering, tears and sin,
Wretchedness of bleak despair.

Slender hands of infant rise,
Reaching to His mother's love;
Sees her smile, endearing eyes,
Image of a gentle dove;

Reassuring presence calms,
Honesty of meekness deep;
Unperturbed by earthly charms,
She in faithful trust will keep

Precious words of God at heart;[3]
Humbled by this calling great,
Chosen, blessed, set apart
To raise a babe divine whose fate

She would rather not discern,
For grief would be too much.
First, the child must grow, learn,
Speak, listen; sense, touch

Anguished needs of those around,
Lives His words and deeds will heal.
Heaven's kingdom sought and found,
Buried pearls of treasure real.[4]

Many others make their choice,
Indifferent to Yuletide's joy;
They of hidden, muted voice
Shun the manger's holy boy.

1. John 3.16; 2. 2 Corinthians 5.19; 3. Luke 2.19; 4. Matthew 6.19-21; 13.44-46

Lost in storms of endless torment,
Hardened by the knocks of life;
God, it seems, does not relent
As they endure recurring strife.

Could it be His wrath outpoured?
Righteous hand unleashing judgement?
Hell on Earth – a just reward?

Baptist John cries out, 'Repent![5]
See the Lamb of God appear;'[6]
One Who comes to seek and save,[7]
Bidding all to Him draw near;[8]
Everything for us He gave.

Temple curtain ripped asunder[9]
Opens up a pathway new;
Freed by Christ through grace of wonder,[10]
Sparing us the sentence due.[11]

Stoke the spiritual fire, imbue
Our longing, ardent glow;
Only You we shall pursue,
Crossing hill and valley low;

Follow where You lead us on,
Hear Your voice, heed Your way.
Fresh streams flowing, deserts gone,
Worship, praise, believe, obey.

Spirit's work shall be complete,
Changing us on steps to glory,[12]
Redeemed, restored, refined, replete,
Lowly bowed as we adore Thee.

Henceforth unto infinity,
God supreme, Lord sublime;
Riding clouds in majesty,[13]
Jewelled crown of honour Thine.[14]

5. Matthew 3.1-2; 6. John 1.29; 7. Luke 19.10; 8. John 6.37;
9. Matthew 27.51; 10. Ephesians 1.6-8; 11. Isaiah 53.4-6;
12. 2 Corinthians 3.18; 13. Deuteronomy 33.26; 14. Hebrews 2.9

Cleaving

Broken pieces, dying, drowned,
Sunset's fading light above;
Heartfelt yearnings frozen-bound,
Snuffed-out thoughts of blissful love.

Like tattered clouds that float away,
Too high to reach and hold,
So are his hopes that once held sway,
Dashed, disillusioned, cold.

Strange events – what can they mean?
All seemed good and right.
Darkness covers what was seen
As daylight turns to night.

Fruitful friendship pure and deep,
Laughter's warming cheer;
Alas, for this I can but weep,
In vain restrain the fear.

Affection's bond, shared delights,
These have brought us nigh;
Flying up like gliding kites,
For more I long and sigh.

It is a lesson hard to learn,
And one that I have tried:
Only for a season's turn
Did we journey side by side.

To those we love we cannot cling,
They are not ours to keep;
Like a bird that soars on wing,
Freedom's gift with zest shall leap.

Sad it is when friends no more
With each other can remain;
Parting leaves such sorrow sore
For hearts that ache and break in twain.

Far and wide my musings wander,
Will I see her ever again?
This and so much more I ponder,
Numbed by melancholy pain.

God's designs are oft unclear
As travel in a foreign land;
I wish He would to me come near,
Gently lead me by the hand.

If only I could comprehend –
He will always walk with me;
Ever-present till the end,
Firm is His fidelity.[1]

Help me live in Your domain,
Stray not from Your ways;
You my comfort, greatest gain
Through hollow, drawn-out days.

Oftentimes Your voice was heard
In prophecy[2] and dream;
Lord, I ask to hear Your word,
Clearly speaking what You mean.

Shattered longings bring despair,
Doubts that I cannot survive.
Yet grace and truth let me declare,
'Spirit, breathe, restore, revive!'[3]

Eyes are lifted to the hills,
Now until eternity;
Help from You my soul infills[4] –
Love's divine serenity.

Inspired, in part, by a sermon on the story of Joseph and Mary in the gospels.

1. Deuteronomy 31.8
2. Hebrews 1.1
3. Ezekiel 37.1-14
4. Psalm 121.1-2

Vitality

I once bought a plant in a vase dark red,
Broad green leaves with pretty white flowers.
'Twas strange one morning when she said,
'I haven't been fed for forty-eight hours!'

Watering can filled to the brim
Brings the plant her longed-for drink;
Smiling, sighing, satisfied grin,
Splashes, sploshes, blink, wink.

Knowing now how much she needs me,
Someone to care, protect, nourish,
Admire, encourage; changes see,
Steady growth of buds that flourish.

Moisture returns her shiny sheen,
Contented mien, richly replenished;
Sparkling eyes, glistening gleam,
Loved, beheld, tended, cherished.

Water and food in bountiful plenitude,
Gulping, gurgling, giggling glee!
Singing in spate of bubbling gratitude,
'Is there a chance that I'll be a tree?'

Wistful ramblings – how long will she live?
Nature's miraculous cycle of life –
Receive, enrich, outwardly give,
Round and round through blessings and strife.

Death inflicts the final blow,
All that breathes will disappear;
Seeds of hope with faith to sow,[1]
Resurrection conquers fear.[2]

1. 1 Peter 1.21
2. Matthew 28.5-6; Hebrews 2.14-15

Soon my plant will be no more,
Wilting transience, fading wish;
Promise affirmed to heal, restore,[3]
World renewed, perfect finish.[4]

Delicate daughter, fragile, clear,
Pure, serene, dressed in white;
Born to the plant, child so dear,
Gift from Fount of love and light.

Opening her heart slowly but surely,
Beauty revealing hidden insides;
Stem supporting firm and securely,
Nurturing Source where she abides.[5]

---

3. Revelation 22.2
4. Revelation 21.5
5. John 15.5

Piano

Single note begins to die
As soon as he is born;
Tone so fine to clarify
His radiating dawn.

Second appears her turn to play,
Third, fourth, trickle to stream;
As sunrise gifts emerging day,
So they stir in nascent theme.

Liquid runs of glinting pearls
Ascend, descend in seamless flow;
Flurries of ornamental whirls
Embellish, sparkling trills aglow;

Fingertips dancing on ivory keys,
Bonded together, harmonious touch.
Silky cantilenas appease,
Soothing the heart's desire for such.

Thunderous octaves powerful, bold,
Torrents unleashed as hammers pound;
Tearing across the keys – behold
Velocity's surging élan unbound!

Clusters' varied shapes and sizes,
Some familiar, others quite new.
Skipping leaps bring novel surprises,
Awkward positions, wrists askew.

Warmth sustained caressing soul,
Pedal's vibrant ring pulsating;
Strings in concord, resonant toll,
Gonging boom of chimes conflating.

Rapid scale, arpeggio
Up and down like silvery drop,
Nimble filigree molto leggiero,
Keyboard spanned bottom to top.

Linear notes moulded, hewn,
Sinuous melodies arch in shape;
Finely spun, impromptu tune
Conjures up beguiling scape.

Harmonies rise from depths below,
Feelings uttered past words' reach;
Plangent chords mutate and grow,
Espressivo songlike speech.

Sounds erupting shockingly raw,
Anguished discords, angry clashes;
Fervent heartstrings now no more
Masked by scars of searing gashes,

Wounds revealing latent needs
Buried under layers of life.
Outburst agitato cedes,
Peace becalms the seething rife;

Music casts her charming strains,
Recomposing spirit's poise;
Mind enthused aspires, attains,
Revels in the fingers' ploys.

Beauty rapt, heard and played,
Priceless gem beyond all measure;
Deepfelt thanks to You be made:
Inspiration, Joy and Treasure.

Out of this World

Grace abundant poured in showers
Raining down most wonderful;
Water's gift for withered flowers –
Thirsty souls, weary, doleful,[1]

Struggling on their way alone;
Hand of God stretching out
Helps them find the path back home,
Leading to that place where doubt

No more leaves its shadowy trace;
Trust unswerving grows secure
Gazing on His kindly face;
Healing balm to gently cure

Sorrows, guilt, ills out-hurled;
Marked by hardship's burning brand,
Tossed by storms, it seems the world
Keeps them from that distant land.

God has made His plans' decree,[2]
None can stop or thwart His will;
Future's promised destiny,
Purposes He shall fulfil.[3]

Final trumpet's brazen call,
Victory of Christ complete;[4]
Every knee shall one day fall,[5]
Worship humbly at His seat;

1. Isaiah 41.17-18; John 4.13-14
2. Jeremiah 29.11
3. Isaiah 55.10-11
4. 1 Corinthians 15.51-57
5. Philippians 2.10

Throne of mercy where He reigns,[6]
Us loved first that we might love.[7]
End of mourning, tears and pains,[8]
King of glory waits above –

This our hopeful expectation;
There we shall with eyes unveiled
Lift our praise in exultation,
See how much His grace availed –

Breadth of scope we cannot grasp,
Past all comprehension lies;
Sacrifice that makes us gasp,
Life surrendered; highest prize

Won for those who to Him turn,
Gain most precious, freely given.[9]
Bathe in wonder, heartfelt yearn,
Knowing that He has forgiven.[10]

---

6. Hebrews 4.16
7. 1 John 4.19
8. Revelation 21.4
9. Ephesians 1.6
10. Ephesians 1.7

Cornucopia

Sweet, wafting scent, grass fresh-mown,
Bright red poppies carpeting field;
Burgeoning berries plumply grown,
Mellow issue of bountiful yield.

Meadows decked with petals' variety,
Colourful shapes of endless extent;
Feast laid out for the eyes' satiety,
Scene idyllic, dreamy content.

Billowing crops tall and fine,
Ready to offer ripened gift;
Basking in the nourishing shine,
Pending harvester's sickling sift.

Lyrical larks on beating wing,
Nature's music soaring high;
Hear them as they live to sing,
Beauty's tones adorning sky.

Ducks on river idling time,
Bobbing in the breezy blows;
Placid motion, rhythmic rhyme,
Casual pace as water flows.

Two of a kind in graceful glide,
Bound as one in lifelong bond;
Gently floating side by side,
Elegant movement, partners fond;

Drifting past the swaying reed,
Cygnets five with downy hair
Follow where the parents lead,
Nurtured with devoted care.

Ladybird flits from stalk to leaf,
Safe inside her speckled dome;
Skimming over tranquil heath,
Seeking spot to make a home.

Herds of curious cattle rest,
Lying, grazing, swishing flies.
Birds full-voiced flying the nest,
Testing strength, mounting to skies.

Great and small sharing the land,
Joined in peaceful harmony;
Held in Plenty's generous hand,
One euphonious psalmody.

Unsurpassed dexterity
Spans imagination's realm;
Utmost skill of creativity,
Stunning vistas overwhelm!

Giver of all delights to bestow
Manifold blessings scattered abroad;
Longing that faith take root and grow,
Bearing fruit of Love adored.[1]

---

1. John 15.5-10

Borderland

Waiting long to be released,
Bodies ailing, bruised and worn;
Wishful thoughts of agony ceased,
Space where dreams can thrive reborn.

Loss of loved ones parted, gone,
Lacerating pangs pierce deep;
Memories tinged with song of swan,
Treasured in the heart to keep.

Dying breath and farewell kiss,
Walking through the shadowed vale;[1]
Will we find Elysian bliss?
Someone there to tell the tale?

Can this foe be ever vanquished?
Satan's hellish hold smashed down?
Those held captive, drained, anguished,
See a stronger Force with crown –

Saviour, Conqueror, death's undoing,[2]
He Whose power no limit knows;
Mighty Source of Life renewing,
Victor over bloodstained gallows;[3]

Final enemy crushed, destroyed.[4]
God's profound, abounding grace
For humankind given, deployed;
Love in action shows His face.

Hard and brutal scourges past,
Free from toil, suffering's mete;
Journey's end in sight at last,
Land of milk and honey sweet.[5]

1. Psalm 23.4
2. Hebrews 2.14-15
3. Acts 2.24
4. 1 Corinthians 15.26
5. Ezekiel 20.6

Once for All[1]

O God enthroned above,
My King and Friend.
To Your far-reaching love
There is no end.
You paid the price for me
At greatest cost;
Your mercy deep I see
Upon the cross.

You bled and grieved for me,
Alone in pain;
Your pardon sets me free –
What perfect gain!
You died and rose again,
Death is defied;
Great Lord on high You reign,
Most glorified.

I shall proclaim this song
With all my heart!
Your presence near and strong
Will ne'er depart.
To You I give my praise
Now and always,
Let grace me so amaze
Throughout my days.

1. Romans 6.9-10

Destitution to Restitution

Naked, weak, helpless, alone,
Harrowed by a hostile world;
Outside shows just skin and bone,
Underneath, a soul upcurled;

Famine's curse leaves scanty sheaf,
Torment's cry for mercy's gain;
Drowning in a sea of grief,
Sense of purpose on the wane.

Women and girls raped in pillage,
Stripped of all their dignity.
Charred remains of home and village,
Carnage brute, vile malignity.

Babies wrenched from mothers' clasp,
Thrown alive into fire of flesh;
Burning humans breathe their last,
Screams of torture's scorching thresh;

Bodies butchered, maimed, aborted,
Stench of death, funeral knell;
Sanity crazed, grotesque, distorted.
Fleeing horror's living hell,

Theirs the nightmare, fateful plight,
Castaway, displaced, distraught;
Forced to run from terror's fright,
Chasmic state of tension fraught.

Going to nowhere, perilous flight,
Desperately seeking site of calm;
Longing for light in perpetual night,
Cease of war's destructive harm.

Selah

Deep within Spirit creates
Tiny seeds of hope to grow;
Rooted Truth regenerates,
Soon His richest fruit to show.

Faith of greater worth than gold,
Fiery trials, refining blaze;
Perseverance steadfast, bold,
Sounding forth with stirring praise.[1]

Father God affirms your hearts,[2]
Helps you stay the rocky course;
Love to you He now imparts,
Guiding lamp from Him the Source.[3]

Life in full abundance free,[4]
Restful gaze at heaven's dawn;
Home of welcome sanctuary,
Haven safe where none shall mourn.[5]

Christ to all shall be revealed,[6]
Glorious as the dazzling sun;
Tribulation's blight is healed,
Justice and salvation won.[7]

Inspired by the sufferings of refugees, and the massacre of Rohingya Muslims in 2017.

1. 1 Peter 1.6-7
2. 2 Thessalonians 2.16-17
3. Psalm 119.105
4. John 10.10
5. Revelation 21.4
6. 1 Peter 1.7
7. Isaiah 51.4-6

Sea of Love

Rolling waves, golden sands,
Deep blue swell, sunlit skies;
Pairs that hold each other's hands,
Symphonies for ears and eyes.

Towering cliffs as giants rise,
Slaty slabs polished smooth.
Rocks of every shape and size
Contrast in their cast and groove.

Crunching pebbles, secret caves,
Twisted lines of strata streak;
Outlines weird entrance the gaze
On the shore of tranquil creek.

Horses white and crested ride,
Galloping with the wind at speed;
Driven by the surging tide,
Once to break and then recede.

Waters meeting edge of land,
Scattered seaweed strewn on beach.
Dunes that undulating stand,
Seagulls perching out of reach.

Dive below, plumb the depth,
Scraggy mountains, gaping trenches,
Wondrous views of awesome breadth,
Undiscovered, fresh adventures!

Vastness of the mighty ocean,
Shining face of power divine;
Longing for our hearts' devotion,
We the branches, You the vine.[1]

1. John 15.5

Deeper than the lowest canyon,
Higher than the tallest peak,
So is Your love; our best Companion,
Everlasting Lord unique.

Inspired by the scenery of the Pembrokeshire coastal path in Wales.

Forever

Leading on with specious lure
In the search for Grail's cure,
Optimism's mirage glows;
How long, how long before he knows?

Bleakness grim, empty despair,
Aimless will devoid of care;
Floundering soul, meagre existence,
Pallid, sagging, lifeless indifference.

Hope is gone. What takes its place?

Selah

Rock of faith whose changeless face
Looks ahead to what will come:
Night must yield to dawning sun.

Plans conceived made in advance,[1]
Guided through each circumstance;[2]
Nestled in redeeming grace,
Lifted up with firm embrace.

Meaning in endurance lies,
Not in worldly profits' prize;
Doing leads astray from being,
Mind impedes the heart's true seeing.[3]

Waiting, Lord, so hard to bear,
Undermining doubts impair.
Though it tarry,[4] not to waver,
Grant him patience in Your favour.

1. Jeremiah 29.11
2. Psalm 48.14
3. Ephesians 1.18
4. Habakkuk 2.3

Thoughts and ways of highest design,[5]
Excellent, lovely, pure,[6] fine
In concept, perfect in form,
Purposed to craft the soul reborn.

Months to years, time slipping by,
Decades viewed in blink of eye.
Thanks be to You, Presence eternal,
Life-inspiring King supernal.

Inspired by R.S.Thomas' poem *Kneeling*.

---

5. Isaiah 55.8-9
6. Philippians 4.8

L

Lilacs	lounging	lackadaisically,
Lupins	leaning	lethargically,
Lilies	lilting	lazily,
Leaves	lisping	leisurely,
Lakes	lapping	loquaciously,
Larks	launching	loftily,
Lambs	leaping	lightly,
Leas	lying	lushly.
Lines	linking	loosely.
Loneliness	liquefying	latently,
Laughter	lubricating	lyrically,
Looks	locking	lingeringly,
Lips	luring	longingly,
Lovers	lavishing	luxuriously.
Lightning	liberating	luminously,
Light	leading	lucidly.
L	*Elle*	L

Llandaff Cathedral

Stately towers of grandeur fine
Framing noble, weighty doors;
Offering pilgrims restful pause
Down the centuries' coursing time.

Enter now this hallowed place,
Let the outside world subside;
Worries and fears allayed; abide.
Feel the moment, present space.

Vast dimensions, spacious scope,
Tombs encasing history's bones;
Massive columns, ancient stones
Built by labourers' concrete hope.

Air with incense sweet imbued,
Portly arches stretching high;
Windows stained in motley dye,
Dimness strange of light subdued.

Choir's wafty tones ascend,
Sonorous notes of pipes ornate;
Haunting chants and psalms elate,
Harmony's striking colours blend;

Range of pitch from depth to height,
Resonant echo, glorious sound;
Vibrant expansion, fullness round,
Glimpsing angels' chorus white.

Rousing hymns, spirits raised,
Minds infused with inspiration;
Joined in chords of exultation,
Christ our Lord, His name be praised!

Evensong

Sky azure, faintest breeze,
Golden twilight orb lies low;
Rays too weak to lift the freeze,
Woods beclothed in orange glow.

Rigid, sombre, naked trees,
Rooted under layers of time;
Branches covered once with leaves,
Unprotected now from rime.

Crispy grass, crunchy mud,
Stagnant streams in ditches dim.
Fields stark drenched by flood,
Scarce a bird on perch or wing.

Glistening cobwebs, clodded earth,
Ploughed-up furrows creviced deep.
Silvery haze of moonlight's birth,
Shimmering beams inducing sleep.

Murky mere in forest glade,
Surface masking hidden bed.
Shadows lurk as daytime's fade
Cedes to dusk's encroaching tread.

Sinking 'neath the pink horizon,
Solar halo ebbs away;
Darkness spreads his mantle iron,
Night arriving, fleeing day.

Paling embers slowly die,
Wispy clouds exchanging hue.
Twinkling stars catching eye,
Sprinkled heavens' generous strew.

Eerie silence steals, becalms;
Echoes past of hectic bustle.
Stillness casts her gentle charms,
Easing inner, tensive tussle.

Blackness lays his mood forlorn,
Cloaked in dragging hours dead.
Spirits long for rising dawn,
Seeking narrow path ahead.[1]

Flares of revelation's flame,
Warmth of true affection kind.
Wisdom's luminescent gain,
Transformation kindling mind.[2]

Light resplendent saves the world,[3]
Triumph over fiend and foe;[4]
Devil's evil powers furled,
Healing won for every woe.

Son of God in sovereign might
Quashed the enemy's wicked schemes;
Vanquished, slain with forceful smite.[5]
Heaven's radiant, blazing gleams

Unsurpassed in glory shine,
Brighter than the sun we see.[6]
Honour, worship, mercy Thine,
Ringing through infinity![7]

1. Matthew 7.14
2. Romans 12.2
3. John 8.12
4. Colossians 2.15
5. 1 John 3.8
6. Revelation 21.23
7. Revelation 7.11-12

Pentecost

Spirit of God breathing power,
Loosing from captivity;[1]
Breaking chains in Satan's tower,
Light in depths where none could see,

Blinded in the dingy gloom,
Senses swamped by tempting urge.
Like a flower in fragrant bloom
Spirit spreads His cleansing purge;

Shaping, honing, gently forming,
Clay in skilful, moulding palms;
Potter's plan is newly spawning,[2]
Life unfolding in His arms.

Do not grieve[3] or quench[4] His being,
Let Him have His way in you;
Shepherd, Helper, Guide all-seeing,
Always He will lead you through:[5]

Times of plenty, deprivation,
Disappointment, hardship, toil;
He, the Way of firm foundation,
Steadfast Friend truly loyal;

Close to us on righteous path,
Resolute in faithful trust.
Purifying fiery hearth
Burns, consuming dross and dust,

1. Isaiah 61.1
2. Jeremiah 18.3-6
3. Ephesians 4.30
4. 1 Thessalonians 5.19
5. Psalm 23.1-4

Substance dead, decayed, dying;
Branches barren stripped away,[6]
Heartfelt groans, deepest sighing.
Inner joy for strength each day,[7]

Spirit's movement soft as breeze,
Else with mighty, roaring gust;[8]
Bathe in silence, wait at ease,
Listen to His whisper hushed.[9]

Ready for works primed in advance,[10]
Destined to accomplish His will;[11]
Gifts bestowed bless and enhance,[12]
Each equipped His purpose to fulfil;[13]

Not alone, but linked as one,
Members of church – bride of Lord;[14]
Persevere to overcome,
Brandishing the Spirit's sword.[15]

Bountiful fruits' alluring appeal:
Patience, kindness, goodness, peace;[16]
Pleasing Him Who longs to seal
Hearts' desires with kiss of release.[17]

Freedom unbound runs His way,[18]
Soul on wing in undreamt flights;
Blessed are they who hear and obey,[19]
Glorify Him with all that delights.[20]

6. John 15.1-6
7. Nehemiah 8.10
8. Acts 2.1-4
9. 1 Kings 19.11-12
10. Ephesians 2.10
11. Ephesians 1.11
12. Matthew 7.11
13. Philippians 2.13
14. Ephesians 5.25
15. Ephesians 6.17
16. Galatians 5.22
17. Psalm 37.4
18. Psalm 119.32
19. Luke 11.28
20. Psalm 37.4; 63.3

Ladybird

Into the room she flew one day,
Finding warmth from the bitter outside;
How long, I wondered, would she stay,
Exploring this strange, new world espied.

I'm curious to know exactly what
This little lady likes to eat;
From seeping plant in earthen pot
Perhaps a juicy, leafy treat?

Crawling along the edge of the bath,
Then on the ceiling sets her sights;
Boldly intrepid forging a path
Further up towards the heights.

Flailing legs, supine she lies,
Desperate, helpless, struggling in vain;
Plucky attempts, always she tries,
Wanting to get on her feet again.

Gentle nudge and all is right,
Relief at last, returning calm;
Sitting tight, no need for flight,
Safe on solid ground from harm.

Water she reaches, stops for a while,
Biding her time in placid repose;
Lapping a drop on shiny tile,
Nourishment pure before she goes

Fearlessly up the slippery wall,
Still unaware of danger below;
Trusting her wings to break the fall,
Teetering near the fateful blow;

Delicate body downwards spinning,
Gravity's force too strong to defy;
Viscous, treacherous grip, sinking,
Feebly trying to once more fly,

Swallowed up by liquid death,
Deep engulfment, no escape;
Energy sapped, gasping breath,
Is this the final, smothering drape?

Quick to the rescue, scoop her out,
Lay her gently down to dry;
Waiting through the anxious doubt,
Hoping that she will not die.

Fading life, motionless,
Tiny, dappled beauty weak.
Tinge of pensive mournfulness
Permeating outcome bleak.

What becomes of creatures all?
Do they rest in fairer climes?
Paradise green for great and small,
Land where sunlight ever shines.

River

Softly moving on his course,
Depth obscure whose progress knows
Steady pull of currents' force,
Through the rolling meadow flows;

Onwards to the distant end,
Destiny as yet unseen.
Channels straight, many a bend,
Banks to hug the glassy sheen.

Swirling eddies playfully spin
Restless in mercurial flux;
Lightly on the surface skim
Looking in towards the crux.

Rapids shallow bubbling along
Chattering merrily on their way.
Soon a place of different song
Heard in tones of mellow sway.

Movement slowed, hovering hush,
Silence of the deepness calm;
Scarce a breeze to stir the rush,
Time held still in tranquil balm.

Lilting reeds in elegant dance,
Charmed by lilies' demure repose.
Foliage floats with nonchalance,
Lazily drifts in peaceful doze.

Weeping willow sheds her tears,
Drooping, bent her body leans;
Wistfulness of many years
Mirrored in the fluid seams,

Glinting 'neath her arching boughs,
Sunlight's quiver speckling leaves;
Tandem ripples gently rouse
Silvery shimmer of fleeting weaves.

Slender trunk, yet strong within,
Roots embedded reaching down.
Creatures of earth and birds on wing
Shelter in her canopy's gown.

Fount of life in welling burst
Watering every inmost need,[1]
Satisfying driest thirst;[2]
Springs of goodness pure exceed,

Overflowing grace outpoured,[3]
Mercy's gift that none may perish;[4]
Healing stream from heaven's Lord,[5]
Ours the choice His love to cherish.

Inspired by the view below of the River Rib at Latchford, Hertfordshire.

1. Philippians 4.19
2. John 4.13-14
3. Romans 5.15
4. 2 Peter 3.9
5. Revelation 22.1-2, 17

Transience

As flowers that bloom then wilt away,
So we are born for just a while;[1]
Hundred years compressed to a day,
Blink of an eye, cursory smile.

Fleeting lives appear like grass,
Blown by wind, gone forever;[2]
Flying hours, months that pass,
Time's erratic whimsies sever

Frail human webs entwined,
Intersecting down the ages.
Striving sense and worth to find,
Chapters of our book on pages

Tell the story of our route,
Mapping out the journey's plan;
Armistice or conflict brute
Marking our allotted span;

Memories of woe and joy
Merging in nostalgic haze;
Fitting chances to employ
Talents bred in gainful ways.

Embryonic seeds are sown,
Patient wait for what shall be;[3]
Steadfast trust as they are grown,
Bearing fruit on verdant tree.[4]

1. Job 14.1-2
2. Isaiah 40.7
3. Romans 8.25
4. Isaiah 55.10-11

Care unfailing He exudes,
Filling us with purpose sure;
Fluctuant vicissitudes
Test and challenge to endure.

Formed by Him, we are but dust,[5]
Fragile in our feeble frame;
Spirit breathes with heartfelt gust,
Souls invoke His hallowed name.[6]

Yahweh's voice encircling time
Makes creation through the Word;[7]
Masterstroke of grand design,
Structure orders chaos absurd.

Infinite realms of mammoth space,
Atoms abounding in life's advance;
Physical states of volatile face,
Whirling eternity's cosmic dance.

Forces' inconceivable might,
Glorious light in darkness dim;
Wisdom's truth to guide aright,[8]
Perfect balance held by Him.[9]

Source divine of all sustaining,[10]
Edifying scheme in motion;
Transcendental power prevailing,
Love profound as deepest ocean.

---

5. Genesis 2.7
6. Matthew 6.9
7. John 1.1-3
8. James 3.17
9. Colossians 1.17
10. Hebrews 1.3

Vision

Misty images, visages blurred,
Swarms of different words and sounds;
Conversations overheard,
Budding thoughts beyond the bounds.

Kaleidoscopic fantasies
Shift and morph in constant flow.
Tender breath of intimacies,
Dormant hopes woken to glow.

Places familiar, others unknown,
Curious sense of déjà vu.
Plans, travels, together, alone,
Arriving, departing, false, true,

Laughs, tears, vanishing echo;
Is it real this world so strange?
Imagination – friend or foe?
Fickle for sure, prone to range

Far and wide at freedom's helm
Across subconscious space so vast;
Lands unmapped in future's realm,
Times recalled from distant past;

Molten mix of changing scenes,
Swirling colours blend their traces.
Sprouting ideas, flowering themes,
Fertile soil of mind's oasis.

Passions inflamed breaking free,
Emotions' heat, flaring seethe,
Inward force of potency
To bind, release, disclose, deceive.

Groping in vain for strands of reality,
Threads of permanent substance to grasp
Between the elusive mutability
Of dreaming and waking; daylight at last.

Spirit indwelling the soul's abyss
Searches, knows all that is hidden;[1]
Holds, unites, with gentle kiss
Heals, restores the broken and riven.

Calm descends after turbulent storm,
Clear perspectives shaped anew;
Light illumes the glimmering dawn,
Dreams decay as memories ensue.

---

1. Psalm 139.1

Spacious Salvation

Spirit of the Sovereign Lord
Anointing with His lavish grace,
Magnified by all, adored;
Reaching out in wide embrace,

Healing lives in turmoil, broken,
Setting captives loose from chain.[1]
Good news to the poor is spoken,
Sight recovered prisoners gain.

Tender gaze, compassion's tears
Long to cure the wounds of old,
Restore the barren locust years;[2]
Let a story fresh be told:

Confidence and faith renewed,
Change transforming deep within,
Stamina by God imbued,
Battles of the Lord to win.[3]

Grounded in the living Word,[4]
Armed to tackle each temptation;
Never forsaken,[5] undeterred,
Helmet worn of firm salvation.[6]

Pillowed soft on waves of love;
Not bestowed with ashes grey,
But beauty's crown from high above,
As night concedes to dawning day.

1. Psalm 107.14
2. Joel 2.25
3. 2 Chronicles 20.15
4. Colossians 2.7
5. Deuteronomy 31.8
6. Ephesians 6.17

Oil of gladness flowing free,
Clouds dispersed in mourning's grief;
Garment of praise in harmony
Lifting souls, despair to relief.

Sturdy, tall, strong they stand,
Rooted fast with gentle sway;
Nurtured by the Father's hand,
Nourished daily as they pray –

Mighty oaks of righteousness
Planted by the Lord, Whose way
Of truth and life[7] vivacious[8]
Splendid glory shall display.

Dedicate the heart's desire,
Seek and strive above all things;[9]
Nothing else can e'er be higher –
Christ exalted, King of kings.[10]

Inspired by Isaiah 61.1-3.

7. John 14.6
8. John 10.10
9. Isaiah 26.8; Psalm 37.4-5
10. Revelation 19.16

Stranded

Sat in a café near passing crowds,
Watching, remote, detached;
Faces blank, like drifting clouds –
Unconnected, unattached.

Automated beings rushing away,
Merged identities, mass anonymity;
Driven by wants, urges of today,
Workaday existence, void superfluity.

Couples estranged eating in silence,
Caught in a web of compliance;
Faked appearance, hollow pretence,
Loveless glare, hostile defiance.

Woman alone, ice cream for comfort
Dousing the pain burning inside;
Keeping composure, guarding the hurt,
Glance averted from others to hide.

Vacant chair, table for two,
Empty space longing to be filled;
Yearning friendship's fondness true,
Empathy's smile, fears bestilled.

Teens addicted to mobile devices
Barely converse or speak at all;
Parents checking emails, prices,
Sending texts, making a call.

Eyes enslaved to lure of screens,
Family groups dismembered, askew;
Contact splitting at the seams,
Ties remaining flimsy and few.

Elderly trapped in isolation,
Single mothers with children's moan;
Needing help in a grim situation,
Struggling for breath, stuck on their own.

Where is the exit from this maze?
Meaningless, angst-ridden life,
Gripping compulsions, latest craze,
Discord's scream of inner strife.

Staring out into distant space,
Lost in mists of vague oblivion;
Left behind in the human race,
Dreaming of Olympus halcyon.

Futile notions, lonely world,
Absent, alien, bereft of cover.

Spirit whispers wisdom pearled –
Closer Friend than closest brother.[1]

---

1. Proverbs 18.24

Arcadia

Beauty leaves me lost for words
In this place I love to be;
Aura blends with song of birds,
Field of charmed tranquillity.

I cannot tell, I know not why
Feelings rise from deep inside;
Tears of bliss I long to cry,
Here for evermore abide.

Flowers of richest, motley hue,
Radiant in their natural glow;
Finest sight displayed to view,
Such array on pristine show.

Hallowed spot, heavenly taste,
Life in Eden's paradise;
Whole in crystal pureness chaste,
Gracious gift of boundless price.

Buttercup, foxglove, daisy bright,
Poppies in dapper attire,
Heads upheld towards the light,
Tapestry divine; admire

This feast, let it ravish!
Flora wears her raiment sheen,
Unrestrained in bounty lavish,
Bathed with effervescent gleam.

Borne aloft on gentle breeze,
Scents of fragrant ecstasy
Captivate with subtle ease;
Swoon in sweet felicity.

Colours' mesmerizing breadth,
Striking scene of nature's art,
Vivid in their tone and depth;
Senses rapt bestir the heart.

All-excelling craftsmanship,
Works revealing mighty hand;[1]
Praise-inspired, heartfelt worship
Now until the Promised Land![2]

Inspired by the Hertfordshire countryside.

1. Deuteronomy 3.24
2. Deuteronomy 6.3

Terminus

Silent lurk, unseen tread,
Creeping murk amongst the dead;
Ghastly shudder, ghostly presence
Round his torpid, icy essence.

Rows of stones, greyish day,
Souls forever gone their way;
Letters faint, shrouding moss,
Long-forgotten sadness, loss;

Stillness hovers all around.
Bodies buried, sacred ground;
Freed from racking pains of life,
Done with earthly troubles rife.

Adults felled in years of prime,
Snatched away before their time.
Children's lives snuffed out at birth,
No more sound of laughter's mirth.

Fragile being, tenuous thread,
Clinging firm in fearful dread;
This our last day could well be,
Morrow's dawn we may not see.

How to spend it if we knew?
Hours remaining precious, few;
Trickling sand passing through
Narrow neck of hourglass, true

To its own unyielding stance,
Measuring out the fading dance;
Stage from cradle to grave is fixed,
Then comes death – chasm betwixt

This world and the realm of heaven,
Else the blackest hell to deaden,
Quenching weight of darkest night.
Reaper Grim with menacing fright

Strikes when often least expected,
Caring not for those affected;
Ripping apart the seams to shreds,
Knowing well that what one dreads

Lies beyond the borders known,
Distant country far from home;
Destined for calamity –
None escapes mortality.

Laid to rest in coffin's fleece;
Choices end, struggles cease.
Theirs the final dwelling place,
Till at last they see His face –

Opening up the passage first,
Threshold crossed with triumph's burst![1]
Looking out for joyful meeting,
Outstretched arms and welcome greeting.

Inspired by the graveyard in Little Hadham, Hertfordshire.

1. 1 Corinthians 15.20, 54-57

Free

Getting up late from dreamy sleep,
No alarm with piercing beep;
Lazy mornings back in bed
Watching films, or read instead.

Eat whatever when you choose,
Quietly sit, leisurely muse,
Playing music for hours on end.
Just yourself; no need to pretend

Or keep up false appearances,
Undisturbed by interferences.
Simply being; no role to perform
Or pressure to fit with the so-called norm.

Masks portrayed to the outside world
Protect the inward frailty furled;
Perception, it seems, is so far away
From reality's truth in clear light of day.

What would it mean for you to disclose
The secret kernel no one knows?
Too much risk it may well be
Letting me cross your boundary.

Selah

No more hiding, timid, afraid.
Love seeks the best in others displayed,[1]
Loosing constraints, healing integrity,
Tenderly melting your vulnerability.

Burgeoning bud of real self,
Jewels rich in spiritual wealth:
Loyal respect, bedrock of trust
Open the floodgates to health robust.

Hear the song of heaven's dove,
Voice affirming from above;[2]
Drawing you closer just as you are,
Warts and all, yet beckoned from far.[3]

Serving others, their needs to meet,
Humbling Himself to wash dirty feet;[4]
Sacrifice made for humankind[5]
Sets you free from burdens that bind.[6]

Run the path of guiding commands,[7]
Ample courage for life's demands;
Heart and mind affixed on Him,[8]
Breathing liberty deep within.[9]

1. 1 Corinthians 13.5
2. Mark 1.9-11
3. Luke 15.18-20
4. John 13.4-5
5. Hebrews 10.10
6. John 8.34-36; Matthew 11.28
7. Psalm 119.32
8. Colossians 3.1-2
9. Galatians 5.1

Bombshell

Terrorist horror blasts the subway,
Innocent lives shattered, deceased;
Fragments of peace melt in the fray,
Groaning planet, despair increased.

Ethnic cleansing, futile bloodshed,
Savage slaughter, firing gun;
Random chance – alive or dead,
Waiting, longing for change to come.

Pointless suffering, needless pain,
Where to turn with no way out?
Fighting to live, efforts in vain,
Clouds descend of darkest doubt.

Where is God in all this anguish?
Where to look? Can He be found?
People abandoned to endless languish,
Waves of buffeting chaos around.

Selah

What if He made Himself known
With self-abased humility?
God Almighty comes to His own
In baby's weak fragility;[1]

Explosive news – miraculous birth
Defying powers of earthly rule;
Love's endeavour shows our worth,
This the first and greatest Yule.

---

1. Isaiah 9.6-7; Philippians 2.5-8

Shining star in dimmest place,[2]
Buzz expectant, bracing start;
Budding prospects brighten apace,
Stirrings within quicken the heart.

Restoration's plan begun,
Tangible grace in flowing motion,
Past all thoughts and dreams far-flung;
Reconciling, healing lotion

Pouring out in brimming measure,[3]
Mending tattered world so broken;
Pays the price for us His treasure,
Unimagined grief unspoken;[4]

Life lived well hung up to die
Bears the crushing punishment;[5]
'Immanuel'[6] – our heartfelt cry,
Mercy triumphs over judgement.[7]

Fully immersed in human plight,
Breathtaking gasp of oneness divine;[8]
Risen victorious to glory's light,[9]
Salvation secured in heaven sublime.[10]

2. Matthew 2.9-10; 4.16
3. Romans 5.5
4. Isaiah 53.7
5. Isaiah 53.5
6. Matthew 1.23
7. Luke 23.33-34; James 2.13
8. Luke 23.46
9. Acts 2.24, 32; Revelation 21.23
10. Revelation 19.1

Standing Firm[1]

We with Him all things can do,
Fortified in every task;[2]
Constant Presence,[3] steadfast, true,
Whate'er He may require or ask.

Faith as small as mustard seed
Mountains into sea can move;[4]
Know His voice, follow the lead,
Shepherd-King His love will prove.[5]

Keeping on the narrow path,[6]
Crossing barren valley bleak;
Guiding hand with sturdy staff,
Rod to comfort us when weak.[7]

Trusting when we cannot see
That for which we long and hope;[8]
Holding to the certainty
Of works foreplanned in wisdom's scope.[9]

Will of God for sure prevails,[10]
Even though the outlook daunts;
Strong defence that never fails
When oppressed by Satan's taunts.[11]

---

1. 1 Corinthians 16.13
2. Philippians 4.13
3. Joshua 1.5
4. Matthew 17.20; Mark 11.22-23
5. John 10.2-4
6. Matthew 7.13-14
7. Psalm 23.4
8. Hebrews 11.1
9. Ephesians 2.10
10. Proverbs 19.21
11. 2 Thessalonians 3.3

Nothing is too hard for Him,[12]
Sovereign rule our lives enfolds;[13]
He foresees the future dim,
Destiny prepares and moulds.[14]

Eagerness for what shall come,
Often promised long ago;[15]
Confident it will be done,
Waiting for the seeds to show;

Yielding crop one hundredfold,
Harvest ripe of actions fine,
Fruit abundant, pure as gold.[16]
Eyes of goodness brightly shine,

Windows to a wholesome heart,[17]
Seeking first the righteous way;[18]
Humbly play the lowly part,
Always His commands obey.[19]

Help us, Lord, in You abide,[20]
Ageless Rock through changing years;[21]
Staying ever by Your side,
Cast on You our cares and fears.[22]

Pressing on to glory's day[23]
Calling us to heaven's dome;
Fragrant words which gently say,
'Cherished friend, My precious own.'[24]

12. Mark 10.27
13. Isaiah 40.10-11
14. Jeremiah 29.11
15. 2 Peter 3.8-9
16. Ezekiel 17.8
17. Matthew 6.22
18. Matthew 6.33
19. Deuteronomy 11.1
20. John 15.4
21. Isaiah 26.4
22. Psalm 55.22
23. Philippians 3.14
24. Jeremiah 31.3; John 15.15

L'Île de Beauté

Détente, repos, sableuses plages,
Gens à l'aise jouant dans l'eau:
Vieux et jeunes de tous les âges,
Grands, petits, minces et gros.

Certains adorent l'éclat du soleil,
D'autres restent à l'ombreux abri.
Brises légères soufflent de la baie
Poussant lentement nuages fleuris.

Enfants criants, riants, barbotants,
Pleins de joie sans aucun souci,
Jetant la balle en bien s'amusant,
Heures contentes de l'après-midi.

Mer turquoise, transparente
Reflète le ciel d'un pur azur;
Douces vagues ondoyantes,
Scintillantes d'une claire allure.

Chaleur humide augmente sans cesse;
Tonnerre lointain annonce son approche –
Grondement bas de colère céleste
Déclenche la foudre d'une force féroce.

Vastes montagnes époustouflantes,
Cimes majestueuses couronnées de blanc;
Belle splendeur impressionnante
Dure à travers le flux du temps.

Île de beauté d'envergure magnifique,
Calme apaisant qui nourrit l'esprit;
Béni par Dieu d'un amour sympathique,
Lieu bienfaisant, oasis de répit.

A translation in free verse is provided on the opposite page.

Corsica

Relaxation, rest, sandy beaches,
People at ease playing in the water:
Old and young of all ages,
Tall, small, slim and large.

Some adore the glare of the sun,
Others stay under shady shelter.
Light breezes blow from the bay
Slowly pushing flowery clouds.

Children shouting, laughing, splashing about,
Brimming with joy completely carefree,
Having a great time throwing the ball,
Hours of pleasure in the afternoon.

Turquoise, transparent sea
Reflects the sky of pure azure;
Gentle, rippling waves
Glittering with bright allure.

Humid heat increases constantly;
Distant thunder announces its approach –
A low rumble of celestial wrath
Unleashes lightning of ferocious power.

Vast, staggering mountains,
Majestic peaks crowned in white;
Fine, impressive splendour
Lasting throughout the flux of time.

Isle of beauty magnificent in scope,
Soothing calm nourishing the spirit;
Blessed by God with kindly love,
Favourable place, oasis of respite.

Reflection

What lies below in deepest mere?
Under naked, curving boughs
Branch protrudes like sunken spear.
Softest breath from wind to rouse

Smoothness of the water's calm,
Mirrored skies and leaves around;
Seldom tones of birds' sweet psalm
Break the numbing void of sound.

Ghosts from distant eras past
Floating midst uncanny ambience;
Fluid in their form uncast,
Odyssey of ceaseless transience.

Phantoms dart like shadowy wisps,
Glimpses brief of spirits fleet
Borne along by time's grey mists,
Quivering shapes with sprightly feet;

Restless in their search to find
Dwelling place, sanctum's peace;
Free from earthly rigours' bind,
Coming home, complete release.

Fading tracks of history's traces,
Judgements made with hindsight's gaze;
Memories faint of far-off places,
Hazy clouds of bygone days.

Murky pond in wooded gloom,
Morbid silence, stagnant grave;
Dank decay, despondent doom,
Waning hopes for courage crave.

Selah

Sun appears between the trees,
Solemn in their ancient stance;
Flickering light, shimmering breeze
Herald the call to swirling dance.

Heaven and Earth rejuvenated[1]
With their Maker one shall be;
Celebration's peals elated,
Grateful hearts give thanks with glee.

His the glory, honour due,[2]
Drawing all unto Himself,[3]
His the Way, the Word so true.[4]
Kissed by Love to perfect health,

Souls at last can find their rest,[5]
Known for who they truly are;
Timeless life at His behest,[6]
Each adorned with crowning star.[7]

Inspired by the scenery of Broom Wood, Essex.

1. Isaiah 65.17
2. Revelation 4.9-11
3. John 12.32
4. John 14.6
5. Psalm 116.7
6. John 6.47
7. 1 Peter 5.4

Dishwasher Ditty

For washing and rinsing I'm a machine,
Saucepans, pots and cutlery;
End the cycle with sparkling gleam,
Shiny, colourful crockery.

When you've cooked and eaten your fill,
Ready I wait to tackle the grime;
Items used to stir, bake and grill,
Others will need to lunch and dine.

Cups and bowls on top must go,
But please remember, upside down;
Water cleans propelled from below,
Doing its work when sprayed around.

Plates on the bottom each other face,
Knives, forks, spoons in the middle sit;
Not overcrowded, as too little space
Leaves things unwashed instead of spick.

Pans should have a jolly good soak,
Especially after a full English fry!
Suds and heat will loosen the yolk,
I do the rest and there's nought to dry.

I must remind you of one thing more:
Before the programme starts to run,
A little white tablet fits into my door
Ensuring the job is properly done.

When I'm finished a beep you hear,
Telling you now it's time to empty;
Stack the cupboards, so racks are clear
For yet more dishes and mugs aplenty.

Spotless and dirty are best kept apart,
A lesson to learn in more than one way.
I, with your help, will do my small part
To keep you healthy in work, rest and play.

Written for the boys of School House, Bishop's Stortford College,
as an encouragement to use the dishwasher!

Load me up and switch me on!

Blessed are the Poor[1]

Struggling, weary, oft they sigh,
Weighted by the constant strain;
Yearn for better times gone by,
Lives in tatters, slashed, slain.

Storms of hate have left their scars,
Aching wounds lie buried deep;
Lingering hurt smoulders, mars,
Tears unshown in hidden weep.

Potent fears of vulnerability,
Driven to seek protection;
Masked appearance jars with reality,
Anxious thoughts of more rejection.

Crying out to God, 'Be kind,
Free us from the trauma great.'
Worn to thread by daily grind,
Cast aside, it seems, to fate;

Suppressed, subdued, dimming glows,
Desolation dwells inside;
Struck, confused by frequent blows,
Fading, forlorn, forced to hide.

Selah

1. Luke 6.20

Now, within, a tiny light,
Trickles of hope begin to flow;
Glimmers of day ending night,
Seeds to sow, dreams to grow.

Expectation's throbbing beat,
Rise, restore what once was lost,
Energy fresh, nimble feet.

Passion's riches at His cost,
Shedding blood as sins were purged,
Cutting grief, heart-wrenched anguish;
Searing stabs of suffering surged,
Left alone in torment's languish.

More than we can ever conceive,
Bountiful love given to all;
Accept, believe, from Him receive,[2]
Hear the voice of Shepherd call,

'Welcome home, dearest child,
Rest yourself in pastures green;[3]
Let me take your burdens piled,[4]
Lead you by the quiet stream.'[5]

Son of God commands and calms,[6]
Souls and bodies fully healed;
He awaits with open arms,
Paradise is now revealed![7]

---

2. John 3.16
3. Psalm 23.1-2
4. Matthew 11.28
5. Psalm 23.2
6. Luke 8.22-25
7. Luke 23.42-43; John 17.3

Apple Crumble in Heaven

Scrumptious spread laid out for all,
Opulence bedecks the hall;
Crops abundant, fruits of flavour,
Bulging platters see and savour.

Each to banquet was invited,
Poor and lowly, rich and knighted.
Places set for those expected,
Not by rank or fame selected;

Chosen by the King of grace,
Judging not by skin or race.
Righteous robes,[1] regal, fine,
Offered free to those who dine,

That none may feel discomfiture,
But rather sense the presence sure
Of Him Whose name inspires those
Who recognise their sin and woes,

Humbly ask for gracious pardon
To walk again in Eden's garden;
Know anew divinity's bliss,
Touched by gentle, sacred kiss.

Host is waiting guests to treat,
Greeting warm as friends to meet.
'Why,' He asks, 'do none appear?
Many were called from far and near.'

Feeble excuses made in haste,
Earthly treasures going to waste.[2]
Now is the time to seize the chance,
Revel in the royal dance!

1. Isaiah 61.10
2. Matthew 6.19-21

How can such a costly gift
Be scorned, refused in callous rift?
Wealth of generosity
Spurned by dull verbosity.

'Are there some to take the place
Of those who would not show their face?
Into the street and country lane,
Fetch the crippled, blind, and lame;

Still there is room, find some more,
Search them out, urge, implore;
Meat and wine enough to sate,
Fill My house before it's too late.'

Seek the Lord while He may be found,[3]
Beware the lie of time unbound;
Come to the feast whilst you are able,
Take your seat at the heavenly table.

Inspired by the Parable of the Great Banquet, Luke 14.15-24.

---

3. Isaiah 55.6

Versus

Heart's desire and reason's sense,
Both with claim to reign supreme;
Battle fraught of wills intense,
Concrete life 'gainst sweeter dream;

How to square these age-old foes?
Deep dilemma rends asunder;
Inner turmoil conflict sows,
Impulse lost to weighty cumber.

Love's élan impels to action,
Urges heave in surging swell.
Logic's cautious, cold retraction
Stemming flow, subduing quell.

Facts of form so plain, objective,
Rooted in their rigid stance.
Feelings tug with force subjective,
Zestful leap to whims of chance.

How can these keep company?
Where to go on road dividing?
Praying for clear epiphany,
Peace of mind assuring, biding.

Choices made that stand secure
In life's chaotic, hectic stress;
Undeceived by fancy's lure,
Eyes on Him[1] Whose tenderness

Nurtures souls, provides support,
Bolsters faith, engenders trust;
Rock unmoving, steadfast fort.[2]
Rest, reflect, attend, adjust,

1. Hebrews 12.2
2. Psalm 62.2

Asking that His will be done.[3]
Insight burgeons lucidly,
Misty doubts dispersed by sun.
Beauty of a spirit free

Following Maker's instruction,[4]
Whatever sacrifice may be;
Overcoming each obstruction,
Plans fulfil our destiny;[5]

Works prepared before to do,[6]
Gifts endowed, strength supplied;
Failure, triumph, many or few,
Blessings poured,[7] temptings defied.

All our thoughts and ways He knows,
Light to lead,[8] Presence to guide;[9]
He, in all the highs and lows,
Stays the same through time and tide.[10]

---

3. Matthew 6.10
4. Deuteronomy 26.16-17
5. Philippians 2.13
6. Ephesians 2.10
7. Malachi 3.10
8. Psalm 43.3
9. John 16.13
10. Hebrews 13.8

Exhilaration

Roaming fells in wild terrain,
Elements vying, shine and rain;
Cycling up to rugged tor,
Thrill of life revealing more.

White-knuckled grip, juddering bars,
Rural lanes, dank, muddy paths;
Wind in hair, refreshing embrace,
Cooling sweat on sun-bronzed face.

Rushing down slopes round corners' bend,
Rough with smooth, tracks without end.
Verdant scapes enchant the eyes,
Wheels whirring, looking to skies;

Flying machines roaring away,
Singing birds' twittering lay.
Mustard flowers' drowsy aroma,
Diadems with glinting corona.

Cricket's lazy match unfolds,
Distant strike of bat on bowls;
Stretched across the yawning hours,
Time to respite yields its powers.

Walkers and riders at casual pace
Saunter, relaxed, far from the race.
Theirs the chance to drink the mood,
Nourish the soul with spiritual food.

Golfers on greens ambling along
Enjoy their game with cares long gone;
High into flight striking the ball,
Frustrated they search – it's too damn small!

Towering giants bestride the shires,
Metal colossi with miles of wires;
Hamlets quaint in sleepy seclusion
Linked to teeming, urban confusion.

Butterflies merrily carried on breeze,
Rabbits at play with mischievous tease
Dashing, scuttling back to their burrow,
Chasing, hiding in field and furrow.

Daisies white, buttercups yellow,
Dandelions reposed and mellow.
Pregnant blossom, branches laden
Clustering in friendly haven.

Leisurely pause, absorbing views;
Rolling downs in lolling snooze
Oozing with seductive charm,
Quieting heart in restful calm.

Beauty of a sky-blue day,
Natural splendour on display;
Marvel of Creator's might
Giving rise to sheer delight!

Broken

Suffocating Earth gasping for air,
Cities lost in filthy smog;
Choking, retching, sick despair,
Lungs polluted, putrid fog.

Chimneys belch revolting fumes,
Waters fouled by toxic trash;
Trees engulfed in smoky plumes,
Ebbing life with cancer's rash.

Forest fires raging wild
Ruining all that lies around;
Fauna flees from den defiled,
Flora burns in scorching ground.

Land and sea besmirched by plastic,
Tainted beauty struggling to breathe;
Legacy of poison drastic,
Caustic chemicals kill and cleave.

Torrid droughts, storms ferocious,
Havoc wreaked too much to bear;
Lives uprooted, blight atrocious,
Grimmest suffering, pleading prayer.

Climate in chaos, utter disarray,
Winter blossom, daffodils' bloom –
Spring too early makes her way;
How to halt our planet's doom?

Can we escape this road to destruction,
Come to our senses, make amends?
Find the balance, healthy construction,
Careful reflection that cures, attends.

Now we must act to save our abode,
Block the imminent peril ahead;
Lighten the weight of crushing load,
That progeny thrive and prosper instead.

This is no dream, but a wake-up call
Before the point of no return;
Urgent remedy ere the nightfall,
Stoke the flame to prompt concern.

Groaning, aching, dying, fragmenting,
Agony's torturous, deadening feel,
Daylight drooping, sombre lamenting.

Selah

Longing to mend, revive and heal,
Looking down on a fractured world;
Creation once so pure and whole,
Precious work of hands that whirled
Moulding all with heart and soul,

Blending as harmonious chord
Ringing out His glorious reign.[1]
Due respect to Him accord,
Magnify His holy name![2]

Alpha in resplendent view,[3]
Restoration soon attained;[4]
Everything again as new,[5]
Omega by all acclaimed.[6]

---

1. Psalm 19.1
2. Isaiah 6.3
3. Revelation 1.8
4. Revelation 22.12-13
5. Revelation 21.5
6. Revelation 5.13

On Top of the World

Massive mountains heavenward soar,
Jagged ridges thrusting high;
Majesty, mystery, grandeur, awe,
Snow-capped peaks caress the sky.

Sweeping gusts of soughing tones,
Glossy pastures, wealth of colour;
Bulky boulders, scattered cones,
Dark-green firs enfold each other.

Wild waters, twisting torrents,
Gaping gorges' gullets gushing;
Cascades' coruscating currents,
Chasms, caverns, roaring, rushing,

Raging, crashing, racing, dashing,
Lashing rocks along the way;
Rainbow shades, playful splashing
Mix with dancing, sparkling spray.

Canyons wide, gullies narrow,
Ever-changing sculpted scenes;
Trickles turn to swirling flow
Forming never-ending streams.

Lakes azure lie still and deep;
Surface ripples, breezes sprightly
Waking baby waves from sleep,
Gently cradled, fondly, lightly.

Valleys lush, long and broad,
Restful rivers wend their course;
Two that merge in twining cord
'Mongst hills enrobed with florid gorse.

Flitting birds and butterflies,
Bees at work with busy humming,
Flowers of myriad tints surprise;
Foretaste brief of heaven stunning!

Fragrance fresh, scented airs
Rouse the joie de vivre within.
Aspirations, fervent prayers
Rising on euphoric wing.

Maker of all enthroned above,
Mightiness Your works declare;[1]
Breadth, length and depth of love[2]
Greater still, beyond compare.

Inspired by the mountain scenery of Austria.

1. Psalm 145.3-6
2. Ephesians 3.18

Aware

Midst the constant, clamouring din,
Life's frenetic, noisy round,
Sense the silent spot within,
Tranquil calm; soft, small sound.

Bathing in the pool of peace,
Centred, focussed, eased to rest,
Grant distracting thoughts release.
Moving inwards on the quest,

Searching for that still oasis,
Far from all the fleet ephemeral;
Beating wings repose in stasis,
Freed constraints of fetters temporal.

Feel your body's ebb and flow,
Taste the present moment sweet;
Breath divine at work below
Blessing, making you complete.

Seeking, waiting, being; seeing
Light illuming pathway clear;
Darkness doused slowly fleeing,
Know His voice in dales drear.

Tread the hallowed ground in awe,[1]
Where may stand the pure in heart;[2]
Contrite too, desiring more
That He may be the greater part.[3]

1. Exodus 3.5
2. Matthew 5.8
3. John 3.30

Tarry for the Spirit's word,[4]
Sifting that which now is heard;
Gifts received, soul bestirred.
Then the belt of truth to gird,[5]

Firmness sure in stormy times,
Battered by the waves of doubt;
As your gaze to heaven climbs,
You will find the means to rout

The evil one, whose tempting snare
Of wicked schemes will lead astray;[6]
Ask the Lord your load to bear,[7]
Filled with power for each assay.

Anxious thoughts to Him be taken,[8]
Cast your cares on Christ supreme.[9]
Sins confessed to be forsaken,
Washed away by cleansing stream[10]

Running down from God on high,[11]
Listening to your pleas' intent;
Daily bread[12] as you draw nigh,[13]
Staying close to Him, content.[14]

---

4. 2 Samuel 23.2
5. Ephesians 6.14
6. Revelation 12.9
7. Matthew 11.28
8. John 14.27
9. 1 Peter 5.7
10. Zechariah 13.1
11. Revelation 22.1
12. Matthew 6.11; John 6.33-37
13. James 4.8
14. John 15.4-5

Final Curtain

When the Day of Reckoning comes,
Clenching terror chills and numbs;
Trumpet blares with thunder peal,
Desperate prayers, 'Please conceal

Your anger's incandescent smite,
Keep us from the endless night;
Spare the last indicting blow,
Let triumphant mercy show.[1]

In Your kindly patience, Lord,
Curb the flashing judgement sword.
As the people grieve, repent,
Stem Your righteous wrath, relent.

Though it breaks Your heart to see
The mess of dire iniquity,
Father God, allow us time
Our will with Yours to realign.'

Wicked thoughts, harmful deeds,
Spiteful words like stinging weeds;
Help us feel the rightful shame,
True remorse for slight of name.

Chastened mind and penitence,
Resolute obedience;
These the goals where sights are set,
Needs by Him are always met.[2]

Lest we cause our own demise,
There cannot be a compromise
'Tween what God asks and what we give;
Honour Him by how we live:

1. James 2.13
2. Philippians 4.19

Loyalty, discipleship,
Constancy of fellowship.
Strength for taxing task provided,[3]
Led with purpose firm and guided;[4]

Walking on the narrow path,[5]
Leaving comfort of the hearth;
Pilgrims through rewards and sorrow,
Presence certain every morrow.[6]

If our hearts to Him be turned,
No fear haunts of being spurned;[7]
Christ received the sentence due,
Vicarious for me and you.

Dearest price, penalty paid,
Greater love was ne'er displayed,
Worthy life laid down for us;[8]
Gospel message sounding thus:

God desires that none shall perish,[9]
Truth for all to know and cherish;
Sin's result is death infernal,
Given to us is life eternal.[10]

Love and justice reconciled,[11]
Scales of equal measure piled.
Piercing wounds from which He reeled
Broke the curse, restored and healed;

---

3. Philippians 4.13
4. Psalm 31.3
5. Matthew 7.13-14
6. Deuteronomy 31.8
7. John 6.37
8. John 15.13
9. John 3.16
10. Romans 6.23
11. Romans 5.8-11

Punished in our place He stood,
Blameless, silent, pinned to wood[12]
By cruel nails ripping flesh,
Bloodstained crown of thorny mesh.[13]

Self surrendered, once for all,
Sufferings which us appal;
Sacrificial death completed,[14]
Sinful stains removed, deleted.[15]

Crushing guilt, failings, dross[16]
Borne by Him upon the cross;[17]
God's dear Son was crucified
That He, the Judge, be satisfied.

Those redeemed by Christ's salvation
Live no more in condemnation;[18]
Freed, forgiven, soul reborn
With Him in everlasting morn.[19]

Listen well to what you hear,
No one knows when He'll appear.[20]
Message of His word is set:
Prepare yourself, do not fret.[21]

Beware the lure of evil mire,
For God is a consuming fire,[22]
Purest white of dazzling holiness;[23]
Let us bow in humble lowliness.

12. Isaiah 53.4-7; Galatians 3.13
13. John 19.2
14. Hebrews 10.10
15. Psalm 103.12
16. Psalm 38.4
17. 1 Peter 2.24
18. Romans 8.1-2
19. John 3.3
20. Matthew 24.36
21. Matthew 24.42; Hebrews 13.6
22. Hebrews 12.28-29
23. Psalm 29.2

Creator's tears from aching heart
Shed for a world torn apart;
Darkness loved instead of Light,[24]
Heinous acts, pervading blight,

Swamping with malicious spread,
Ruthless hate, increasing dread;
Innocents poor, trapped, languishing,
Hopes and dreams slowly vanishing.

Living hell's incessant course,
Satan's unremitting force
Defying the Almighty's reign,
Humanity's pernicious bane;

None can overrule God's hand,
Numbered days of hourglass sand
Bring to end the devil's hour,
Burning lake will him devour.[25]

Soon shall come a time to view
Heaven and earth reformed anew;[26]
Death and mourning passed away,[27]
Immanuel – henceforth, alway.

River of life from celestial throne,
Crystal clear, gift inflown;[28]
Leaves of the tree healing nations,[29]
Alleluias, celebrations![30]

---

24. John 3.19; 8.12
25. Revelation 20.10
26. Revelation 21.1
27. Revelation 21.4
28. Revelation 22.1, 17
29. Revelation 22.2
30. Revelation 7.9-12

Just a Second

The past is a story beyond all changing;
The future is a dream of infinite ranging;
The present is a gift – moments engaging.

Fall and Rise

Single flake of form unique
Floating down, feathery, meek;
Cushioned gently on the ground,
Gratified its place is found.

Others on the pane they sit
Melting slowly drip by drip;
Drops that move to plop again
One day will return as rain.

Quivering shapes dance and drift,
Buoyed on currents' tender lift;
Playing in their zesty scurry,
Wildered mass of frolic flurry.

Blanket's depth of softest fluff
Covering over all the rough;
Landscapes new becharm our gaze,
Powdered trees with frosty glaze.

Brightest lustre, spotless, whole,
Purest essence deep in soul.
Each its path must firmly take,
Travelling light, repudiate

That which may impair, restrain.[1]
Face the winds which wax and wane,
Leave the safety of the cloud,
Inspiration's zeal endowed

By One Who walked the harder way;[2]
Perfect love keeps fear at bay.[3]
He as man was sent to Earth,
Humanity in fullest worth;

Lowly was His story's start,
Lived and played the humble part;
Life renounced for every friend[4]
So we assured to Him may wend.

Spirit divine in body's frame,
Born to die for sinners' gain;
Loose the trapped from vicelike snare,
Captives free from dingy lair.[5]

Scarlet sins made white as snow,
Crimson red to woolly glow;[6]
Heart of stone is now replaced
With one of beating flesh engraced.[7]

Came to seek and save the lost,[8]
Gave Himself at utmost cost;[9]
Goodness poured with magnanimity[10]
Rescues us for all eternity.

1. Hebrews 12.1
2. Matthew 7.13-14
3. 1 John 4.18
4. John 15.13
5. Isaiah 61.1
6. Isaiah 1.18
7. Ezekiel 36.26
8. Luke 19.10
9. Titus 2.13-14
10. Psalm 145.7-9

Dying to Live

Stripped, barren, vulnerable, bare,
Fading gloss of efflorescence;
Desolate sadness, bleak despair,
Waning loss of effervescence.

Sap sucked out from sickly roots,
Thinning flow of deliquescence;
Stunted, shrivelled, downcast shoots,
Dimming glow of luminescence.

Twinging creak of branches brittle,
Weathered bark, torn and bruised;
Fallen leaves to nothing whittle,
Glory's shadow faint, diffused.

Troubles borne with valiant heart,
Hostile forces' cruel spite;
Years of playing the noble part,
Changing scenes in varied plight.

Footing sure on solid ground,
Integration formed within;
These adorned her beauty crowned
Shining bright with radiant vim.

Place of friendship, comfort, rest,
Creatures knew this home and bed.
Birds now lacking sheltered nest;
Tattered twigs, rotten, dead.

Other trees she sees nearby,
Lavish parade, finest green;
Reaching up towards the sky,
Vigour in their youthful sheen.

Weeping heart in spate of grief;
Loneliness cuts deep inside,
Longs to move and find relief,
Make the gnawing pain subside.

Rocklike form of permanence
Overpowered by raw abrasion;
Upright, bold resilience
Wilting into degradation;

Ravage harsh of brutal time,
How much more can she endure?
Dreams of paradise sublime,
Bliss of water's salving cure.[1]

Crossing fields on his way,
Louring axeman's fateful tread.
Trembling panic, fright, dismay,
Span expired, depleted, bled;

Mighty trunk is felled by blows,
Ever closer nearing death;
Embers dulling, ebbing throes,
Torment ceased with final breath.

Selah

---

1. Isaiah 12.3

Far below in darkest earth
Something small begins to stir;
Tiny seeds' erupting birth
Surging fresh in throbbing spur;

Great potential, life reborn,
Wheel of existence turning;
Energy's source, plenty's horn
Blazing forth now affirming:

Old has gone, new has come[2]
Generating re-creation;
Unimagined things begun[3] –
Liberating transformation!

Inspired by the view below at Launde Abbey, Leicestershire.

2. 2 Corinthians 5.17
3. Isaiah 43.18-19; 1 Corinthians 2.9; Ephesians 3.20

More than Conquerors[1]

No temptation ever too great,[2]
Persevere through thick and thin,
Dwell in Him with patient wait.
Fight the battles, aim to win,

Fix your eyes on Him Who won[3]
The crucial conquest; fallen foe,
Evil's legion smote, undone,
Crushed by Love's triumphant blow.[4]

Never will it be too tough
To find a way and overcome;
During times of hard and rough
Shines behind the clouds the sun.

Resist the devil, watch him flee,[5]
Take your stand against his schemes.[6]
Christ-infused authority
Quells the dark with lucent beams.[7]

Satan prowls like roaring lion,[8]
Do not fear or take retreat;
Armour's plates, protecting iron
Give you strength for his defeat:

Belt of truth around your waist,
Breastplate firm of righteous heart;
Bravely seize the shield of faith,
Douse the flaming arrows smart.

1. Romans 8.37
2. 1 Corinthians 10.13
3. Hebrews 12.2
4. Colossians 2.15
5. James 4.7
6. Ephesians 6.11
7. John 1.4-5
8. 1 Peter 5.8

Helmet of salvation sure,
Word of God – Spirit's sword;[9]
Holiness of living pure,
Worship Him as One adored.[10]

Keep alert and always pray –
This your foremost weapon is.[11]
Stay the course by night and day,
Treasured child – you are His.[12]

Lucifer with cunning stealth
Plots to harm your soul, devour;[13]
Look to God to guard your health,
Steadfast on the Rock of power.[14]

Though the onslaught may be fierce,
He will never leave your side;[15]
Follow Him through vale of tears,
Trust as you in Him abide.[16]

Every thought be captive taken
In obeyance to the King.[17]
Worried, stressed, broken, shaken,
Harboured in His arms you cling.[18]

Beware enticements' subtle lure,
Persuasive in deceptive guise;
Self-control keeps you secure,
Light of goodness fills your eyes.[19]

9. Ephesians 6.10-17
10. Psalm 29.2
11. Ephesians 6.18
12. 1 John 3.1
13. 2 Corinthians 11.14; 1 Peter 5.8
14. Psalm 62.2
15. Joshua 1.5
16. John 15.4
17. 2 Corinthians 10.5
18. Deuteronomy 33.27
19. Luke 11.34

Christ was tempted just as we,
Urges of the flesh He knew;
Yet sinless stayed in sanctity,[20]
Testing lies He cut right through.[21]

We do not live by food alone,[22]
But also on the bread of heaven.[23]
He Who holds us as His own[24]
Knows our hurt and sorrows leaden.

Heavy-laden, weary, sad,[25]
Touch His presence when distressed;
Peace of mind and hearts made glad,[26]
Enter into His sweet rest.[27]

Guiding us towards His throne[28]
Joy's unending life to spend;[29]
Prospect of the promised home[30]
Greeting us at journey's end.

---

20. Hebrews 4.15
21. Matthew 4.1-11
22. Matthew 4.4
23. John 6.33
24. Psalm 139.7-10
25. Matthew 11.28
26. John 14.27
27. Hebrews 4.10-11
28. Psalm 48.14
29. Psalm 16.11
30. Deuteronomy 6.3

Boundless

Praise exultant, cheerful voice,
Souls uplifted swell, rejoice,
Keen to pave the season's way;
Winter knows he cannot stay.

Snowdrops gather in their throng
Bursting forth with merry song.
Daffodils in youthful zest
Flaunting halo effloresced.

Streams of living water quench
Wastelands with abundant drench.
Linger not on former things,
See the new leap up on wings[1] –

Eagles soaring, graceful flights,[2]
Swooping down to novel sights;
Untapped well of full potential
Grounded in the reverential

View of His encircling strength,
Limitless in breadth and length;[3]
Pearls exceeding all conception,[4]
Blessings showered with affection.[5]

Freed from shackles holding fast,[6]
Gripped no longer by the past.
Through the desert forge a trail,[7]
King approaching – let us hail!

1. Isaiah 43.18-19
2. Isaiah 40.31
3. Ephesians 1.19-20
4. Matthew 13.45-46
5. Ephesians 1.3
6. John 8.36
7. Isaiah 40.3

Vital Source of primal might,
Healing glow with gleaming white;
Rhythmic step in vibrant dance,
Rhapsody of vernal prance!

River's bounty, brimming delight,[8]
Darkness scattered, brilliant Light;[9]
Fountain feeding spirit's life,[10]
Nurturing like man and wife.

His the most compelling story,
Gracious gift of godly glory.
Hearts aroused and buoyed afresh,
Spring arrives in sparkling dress!

8. Ezekiel 47.7-12
9. John 1.5
10. John 4.14

Being

Sense   the stillness.

Inhale   the peace.

Live   the moment.

Exhale   the sighs.

Notice   the thoughts.

Centre   the breath.

Embrace   the soul.

Solace   the heart.

Breakout

Easter Day – Christ is risen!
Resurrection force awakes.
Freed from Satan's darkest prison,
Chains of crushing death He breaks;

Loosed from earthly ties at last,
Out of grave to life renewed.
Dumbstruck faces all aghast,
Body raised, no more entombed;

Startling mystery – He was dead.
Strung up high and crucified,
Wounded, scourged, pierced, bled,
Stricken, smitten, suffered, died.[1]

This, it seemed, the dismal ending,
Disillusioned followers fled;
Smothered by despair and bending
Under strain of nervous dread.

Then the best surprise of all
Far beyond our expectation;
Witnesses who hear Him call,
Joyful news for hearts' elation.[2]

'Can it be? Is it true
What He said has taken place?'
'Look for yourself! Tomb in view,
Vanished corpse, vacant space.'[3]

1. Isaiah 53.3-6
2. Matthew 28.8-9
3. Luke 24.1-7

God will have the final word,
Plans fulfilled accordingly;[4]
Sovereign power on Christ conferred,[5]
Serving in humility.[6]

Worldly rulers bow the knee,
Recognise God's Son encrowned,[7]
Glorious in His majesty.
Mercy with compassion bound,[8]

Greatest Friend, highest price[9]
Paid to set us free from sin;[10]
Perfect, noblest sacrifice,
Lives to save, souls to win.

---

4. Isaiah 55.11
5. Daniel 7.13-14; Ephesians 1.19-20
6. Mark 10.45; John 13.5
7. Philippians 2.5-11
8. James 5.11
9. John 15.13
10. Romans 8.2

Transplant

Heart of caring tenderness –
Verdant lea in bloom complete,
Changed to dusty wilderness
Withered by the parching heat;

Arid, cracked, hard as bone,
Rigid casing, unreceptive;
Locked in casket on its own,
Sealed in to stay protective.

Struggles fraught extract their toll,
Flee to safety, hide, withdraw;
Tossed about like ragged doll,
Drowning in emotions sore,
Hurt so many times before.

Selah

Striving for the sense and means
To cope, flourish, find the shore
Stretching out to untamed dreams;

Hope rekindled free to thrive,
Watered by the streams of Love,[1]
Sourced by heaven's sweeping drive.
Gentle touch of soothing Dove[2]

Gives pulsing life and spirit new,[3]
Born again to purpose, meaning.
Leave the prior, chafing rue,
Turn instead to future's teeming

Fertile buds emerging soon,
Endless scope of possibility;
Chances rich and opportune,
Open chest of creativity.[4]

Choicest blessings' full supply,[5]
Font of kindness overflows;[6]
Lord and Saviour, hear our cry,
Grant us faith that boldly shows

Trust in You, all-seeing Guide,
Leaning not on understanding;[7]
Steer us cross the ocean wide
Till we reach the distant landing.[8]

1. Isaiah 44.3
2. John 1.32
3. Ezekiel 36.26
4. Isaiah 43.18-19
5. Malachi 3.10
6. Isaiah 63.7
7. Proverbs 3.5
8. Psalm 48.14

Pilgrim

Wondering where it may be found –
Space we long to call a home;
Nest in which the self unbound
Truly feels its essence own.

Searching often far and wide,
Ceaseless quest for restful dell;
Put the bitter trials aside,
Calm the soul's disturbing well,

Seek the stillness of the core,
Inner sanctum's deep tranquillity;
Learn to shut the outer door,
Barring shallow superfluity.

Striding up to giddy heights,
Mountain peak and coastal scene –
Preview of celestial sights,
Frisson pure, vista serene;

Beauty on such stunning scale,
This could be Elysium's field,
Were it not for human wail,
Cleaving sword of conflict's wield.

Here we have no resting place,[1]
Just a worldly passing-through;
Fragile body, name and face
Closely known by precious few.

1. Hebrews 13.14

Never fully comprehended,
Lonely in the secret parts;
Wanting needs left unattended,
Minds unblossomed, broken hearts.

Looking for the real abode,
Where that lies who can say?
Wandering nomad on the road,
Find this jewel's glinting ray.

Selah

Way and Truth,[2] living Word,[3]
He for us the journey made,
Resolute and undeterred.[4]
Firm foundation readied, laid,

Splendid mansion, rooms profuse
Primed for us His offspring.[5]
Coming home from toil and bruise,[6]
Welcomed by the Father-King;

Folded in His warm embrace,
Final dwelling, land secure;
Life eternal,[7] house of grace,
Peace surpassing ever sure.[8]

---

2. John 14.6
3. John 1.1-4, 14
4. Hebrews 12.2
5. John 1.12-13; 1 John 3.1
6. John 14.2-3
7. John 3.16
8. Philippians 4.7

Index of Titles

Apple Crumble in Heaven	74
Arcadia	56
Aware	84
Being	99
Blessed are the Poor	72
Bombshell	62
Borderland	30
Boundless	98
Breakout	100
Broken	80
Cleaving	20
Cornucopia	28
Destitution to Restitution	32
Dishwasher Ditty	70
Divine Loves	9
Dying to Live	92
Evensong	40
Exhilaration	78
Fall and Rise	90
Final Curtain	86
Forever	36
Free	60
Just a Second	90
L	38
Ladybird	44
L'Île de Beauté	66
Liquid Lament	14
Llandaff Cathedral	39
Majesty	6
More than Conquerors	95
Once for All	31
On Top of the World	82
Out of this World	26
Pentecost	42
Piano	24

Pilgrim	104
Reflection	68
River	46
Sea of Love	34
Shadowland	12
Spacious Salvation	52
Standing Firm	64
Stranded	54
Swiftness Never Ceasing	16
Sylvan Scape	10
Terminus	58
Transience	48
Transplant	102
Unwrapped	18
Versus	76
Vision	50
Vitality	22

Index of First Lines

As flowers that bloom then wilt away	48
Beauty leaves me lost for words	56
Bluebells spread out far and wide	10
Broken pieces, dying, drowned	20
Détente, repos, sableuses plages	66
Easter Day – Christ is risen	100
Empty plains of hours stretch long	12
Father sent His only Son	18
For washing and rinsing I'm a machine	70
Gates of heaven open wide	6
Getting up late from dreamy sleep	60
Grace abundant poured in showers	26
Heart of caring tenderness	102
Heart's desire and reason's sense	76
Into the room she flew one day	44
I once bought a plant in a vase dark red	22
Leading on with specious lure	36
Lilacs lounging lackadaisically	38
Massive mountains heavenward soar	82
Midst the constant, clamouring din	84
Mighty pillars, towering, bold	16
Misty images, visages blurred	50
Naked, weak, helpless, alone	32
No temptation ever too great	95
O God enthroned above	31
Praise exultant, cheerful voice	98
Roaming fells in wild terrain	78
Rolling waves, golden sands	34
Sat in a café near passing crowds	54
Scrumptious spread laid out for all	74
Sense the stillness	99
Silent lurk, unseen tread	58
Single flake of form unique	90
Single note begins to die	24
Sky azure, faintest breeze	40
Softly moving on his course	46

Spirit of God breathing power	42
Spirit of the Sovereign Lord	52
Stately towers of grandeur fine	39
Stripped, barren, vulnerable, bare	92
Struggling, weary, oft they sigh	72
Suffocating Earth gasping for air	80
Sweet, wafting scent, grass fresh-mown	28
Terrorist horror blasts the subway	62
The past is a story beyond all changing	90
Waiting long to be released	30
Welling up from deep within	14
We with Him all things can do	64
What is this thing that we call love?	9
What lies below in deepest mere?	68
When the Day of Reckoning comes	86
Wondering where it may be found	104

~~~~~~~~~~~~~~~~~~~

Acknowledgements

I am grateful to the following for their contribution and support:

- John Bladen and Wendy Jennings, for proofreading the poems (www.wendyjenningscreative.co.uk);
- Reverend Amanda Duncan, for reading through the poems and writing the back cover precis;
- Ian Morris, for suggestions and proofreading the poems;
- Anne Picton, Margarita Webb and Bill Dyson, for suggestions and proofreading the poem *L'Île de Beauté*;
- Reverend Steve Clark, for suggesting the title of the poem *Spacious Salvation*;
- Chris Sutherland, for the front cover design and editing of photos;
- Ian Taylor, for the photo on page 11;
- Pixabay.com, for the photos on the front and back cover, and those on pages 57 and 83;
- John Barfoot and the staff at CZ Design & Print, for their patient assistance during the editorial process;
- All those who have encouraged me along the way.

Biography

David grew up in rural Buckinghamshire and was educated at Stowe School and Durham University, where he studied music and qualified as a teacher. Subsequently he took a degree in languages and taught French, German and music for many years in various schools. Since 2013 he has been the Musician in Residence at Bishop's Stortford College in Hertfordshire, where he gives instrumental lessons, as well as rehearsing with pupils for their exams and concerts. As a pianist he enjoys performing chamber music and accompanying. He is also a keen organist who plays for services at local churches. Favourite pastimes include hillwalking and cross-country cycling.